D1524115

The Horse That Saved the Union

The Horse
That Saved
the Union

*   *   *   *   *

A True Tale of the American Civil War
for Young Readers

by

B. D. Slawter

Bruce D. Slawter

ISBN-13: 978-0692302767

ISBN-10: 069230276X

Library of Congress Control Number: 2015904550

Blue Eagle Books
Springfield, Virginia

To Forrest, Gavin, Madelyn, and Penelope –

*May you always find inspiration from our past,
as you seek your own life adventures.*

CONTENTS

MAPS

IMAGES

Foreword for Parents and Teachers

The Battle of Cedar Creek, which took place on October 19, 1864 – 150 years before this historical narrative was first published – resulted in the loss of nearly 9,000 Americans killed, wounded, or missing. The significance of this number becomes apparent when considering the fact that, during the American Civil War, the U.S. population (31 million) was about ten percent of what it is today (approximately 316 million). Thus, one can conclude that the losses on this single day back in 1864 touched proportionately more American families than all U.S. military losses in the first 13 years following a more recent trans-formative event in our nation's history – the attack on the World Trade Center on 9-11. Yet, by Civil War standards, Cedar Creek was just a medium-sized battle. Another interesting comparison is that 21 Americans (all Northerners) won the Congressional Medal of Honor for their heroic actions on that day – an amazingly disproportionate number for any Amer-ican military operation, both before or since the battle.

These statistics aside, what makes the Battle of Cedar Creek and the accomplishments of Union General Philip H. Sheridan and his horse Winchester particularly worth remembering are the implications of what might have happened to the United States had these main players in our story not ridden onto the field of battle during that fateful day. Would Abraham Lincoln's re-election (about three weeks later) – which seemed assured the previous month after the fall of the Southern stronghold of Atlanta – have been placed in jeopardy? Moreover, would Lincoln's opponent,

George B. McClellan, having then achieved a narrow electoral victory as a result of a surprise Southern triumph, have let the Confederacy go its separate way?

Lincoln himself had expressed doubts about his prospects for re-election just two months earlier, as Union armies became bogged down in a slugfest around Richmond and Petersburg in Virginia.

On August 23, 1864, Lincoln shared with his cabinet members a contingency memorandum, in which he noted that he would probably *not* be re-elected by the war-weary North.* He therefore sought the pledge of his department heads to work with the incoming McClellan Administration to pursue with particular vigor his principal wartime objective of forcing the rebellious South back into the Union – before inauguration day, the following March.†

This solemn pledge from his cabinet heads to continue military operations during the lengthy transition period was necessary, Lincoln explained, because McClellan could not prosecute the war after being officially sworn in as President – due to his campaign pledge to seek an immediate peace with the Confederacy after his inauguration.

Although Lincoln's mood was buoyed by the surrender of Atlanta several weeks later, there was no

---

* Most accounts of this episode add that Lincoln was so worried about losing the election that he even asked his cabinet heads to sign the memorandum sight-unseen.

† Presidential inaugurations would only be moved up from March 4th to January 20th (its current date) with the ratification of the 20th Amendment in 1933. Therefore, in 1864, the transition period between an outgoing Lincoln Administration and an incoming McClellan Administration would have been nearly four months – a critically long period during that stage of the Civil War.

significant change in the key military theater of Virginia. As the first shivers of a chilly fall descended upon the nation's capital, casualty reports from Union trenches around Richmond and Petersburg continued to flow in. In addition, Confederate General Jubal Early's under-strength army in the Shenandoah Valley still posed a threat to Washington, D.C.; and there were rumors that General Robert E. Lee was sending re-inforcements to Early in an eleventh-hour effort to seize the Northern capital.

The Union victory at Cedar Creek secured Lincoln's re-election. Sheridan and Winchester went from relative obscurity to "rock-star" status almost overnight. This phenomenon can be explained by the sad reality that most folks living in the North in late 1864 (more so, perhaps, for those living in the South) were worn out by the war, both in terms of the human losses and the socio-economic costs. People were eager for good news and hungered for real-life heroes who could give Americans hope for the future. For American children living in the North, Winchester the horse – the animal part of the warrior-warhorse team – became the equivalent of Rin-Tin-Tin and Lassie, all rolled up into one lovable animal.

For nearly 50 years after the battle, "Sheridan's Ride" – a second-rate poem written by an otherwise undistinguished poet, Thomas Buchanan Read, just days after the battle – could be seen hanging in classrooms throughout the North; and students were taught to recite its lines. The fact that both characters, "Little Phil" Sheridan and his spirited horse Winchester, were initially pegged as misfits, and that their story had a classical American rags-to-riches feel to it, only served to accelerate their meteoric rise to fame.

The passage of Sheridan and his horse from the real world of historical fact into the mythology of American folklore was furthered by additional symbols of popular culture at the time: a jaunty little ballad written to accompany the poem first penned by Read; several paintings composed by Read himself, who was a better artist than he was a poet; a military march written by the famed John Phillip Souza; and finally, a magnificent monument created by up-and-coming sculptor Gutzon Borglum. Borglum would move on to his far better-known achievement carving out the heads of Presidents from Mount Rushmore – but only after unveiling his stunning bronze representation of Sheridan and Winchester to an admiring President Theodore Roosevelt and a large crowd of Civil War veterans in November 1908. "Teddy," whose rise to the highest office of the land was propelled by his own military exploits charging up San Juan Hill during the more recent Spanish-American War, dubbed the statue as "First-Class."

* * * * *

As this is the author's first foray into the field of Children's Literature, he is very grateful for the advice of several experts, who took the time to read an earlier version of the manuscript and made useful suggestions as to how the author might best introduce this story of the Civil War to a new generation of young readers.

First and foremost, the author sought the advice of his wife Suzanne Slawter, a veteran school teacher with 26 years of experience teaching children how to read, who provided the author with a number of important editorial recommendations and put him in contact with colleagues who cover the Civil War in some detail during the sixth grade in Virginia schools. One of these curriculum experts was Alice Mayoral, who provided badly needed feedback as to how to connect with young readers; and she also explained how the Civil War is taught today in Virginia schools. Forrest Chilton, also a sixth-grade general education teacher who covers the Civil War, provided additional recommendations. Dawn Page, a literacy specialist, evaluated the appropriateness of the terminology for students, provided useful feedback and thoughtful encouragement – and suggested the glossary.

Gerard W. Gawalt, a nationally acclaimed historian specializing in America's founders, now retired from the Library of Congress (LOC) but who continues to author scholarly but highly readable books about the nation's beginnings, provided ongoing encouragement and advice as to the publishing field. Dr. Gawalt also pointed the author toward the comprehensive on-line reference resources located on the LOC's website.

Reference librarians throughout the region, most notably at the small but mighty Fauquier County Library in Warrenton, Virginia, were key in locating rare primary sources, such as an original edition of the *Personal Memoirs of P.H. Sheridan, General, United States Army.*

Lastly, the author would like to thank British sculptor Tessa Pullan for her permission to reproduce for this book an image of her beautiful bronze monument, *Civil War Horse,* which is located outside the National Sporting Library and Museum in Middleburg, Virginia, the epicenter of Thoroughbred country.

* * * * *

While this narrative focuses on the key events in the lives of General Sheridan and his horse "Rienzi/Winchester," the story does take place within the context of the American Civil War. The author's underlying motive therefore is to get young readers interested in the Civil War itself; and furthermore, to foster a more in-depth discussion between students, parents, and teachers as to what the war was all about – beyond the usual sound-bites – to include a dialogue about the causes of the conflict (noting the prominent role of the problem of slavery), wartime objectives (something quite different than "causes"), and the perspectives of those Americans living in the two principal regions of the country at the time.

Beyond fostering a general interest in this period of U.S. history, the author hopes that this and other stories about the Civil War will challenge the student to appreciate the rudiments of campaign strategy, and how it does or does not support political outcomes, including at times elections here in the United States.

As the basic motive for writing this narrative is to give students a peek into the treasure trove of stories and truths about ourselves that can be discovered by reading about the Civil War, the author's instinct is to face several thorny issues related to the period head on. Thus, the narrative does not buck away from controversial themes – such as the notion that the gut-motive of the common man fighting on both sides might have been as simple as to preserve the "Spirit of 1776"; that the slavery question – the primary ingredient in the explosive dispute between North and South – wasn't as "cut and dry" in 1861 as its seems today; and that Lincoln did not initially (or even perhaps primarily) prosecute the war to do away with slavery. Some may disagree with this approach of injecting such controversial or complex issues into a story written with young readers in mind.

Limiting the narrative to just the bare bone events in the life of Sheridan's horse (and to tell the tale solely from the animal's perspective) – as some might prefer – could very well keep students engaged during a single reading of the book. However, the author believes that to prune off the larger context of the war itself would be to miss the point altogether. Having given a number of talks on the Civil War to audiences of all ages, the author believes strongly that any telling of the conflict needs to have a discussion of these hot topics up front; and if explained in plain language, with a balanced appreciation for those living in the past, audiences of all ages can grasp the main themes without undue confusion or prejudice.

Hopefully these issues of historical context, which are introduced after the two main characters get to know one another, will be viewed as central to the story; and their brief coverage will add to a greater appreciation of the characters' accomplishments, without distracting or discouraging the young reader.

* * * * *

To help foster a discussion of the story and the Civil War between students, parents, and teachers, the author has included some suggested discussion questions (and possible answers) – after a glossary of terms – plus a list of additional resource materials for further reading.

Moreover, it is the author's hope that young readers, families, and school classes, particularly those residing within an hour or two of our nation's capital, might find the opportunity to visit the locations or view the artifacts mentioned in this story.

First on the list of places to visit would be the Cedar Creek Battlefield itself, located near the village of Middletown, Virginia, just several miles to the north of the intersection of I-66 and I-81 (a 90-minute drive from Washington, D.C.). While this beautiful Shenandoah Valley battlefield is accessible throughout the year, the Cedar Creek Battlefield Foundation and Belle Grove Plantation host a large-scale re-enactment and living history on the anniversary of the clash, faithfully each October. The event is one of the very few of its kind that is still permitted to be staged on the very field of battle where the fighting took place.

Closer to Washington, D.C., at the National Sporting Library and Museum, located in beautiful Middleburg (not to be confused with the Middle*town* mentioned above), is Tessa Pullan's sad but beautiful monument paying homage to the forgotten horses and mules who gave their lives in support of Union and Confederate armies during the conflict.

Three artifacts mentioned in this book are located in downtown Washington, D.C., itself. Read's iconic oil painting of Sheridan and Winchester (based upon the artist's poem, "Sheridan's Ride") can be viewed in the Smithsonian's National Portrait Gallery; and Winchester himself, thanks to the respectful preservation efforts of 19th Century taxidermists, can still be seen in all his glory in the Smithsonian's National Museum of American History, located on the Washington Mall.

Last but not least for this would-be scavenger hunt is Borglum's bronze statue of Sheridan and Winchester (the photo featured on the cover of this book), which is located in the center of a round-about on Massachusetts Avenue, aptly named "Sheridan Circle." The famed sculptor's monument represents a radical artistic departure from many other statues of military heroes in the nation's capital, which tend to feature riders calmly sitting on their resting horses. By contrast, Borglum's work depicts rider and warhorse as one unified force in motion – Winchester sliding majestically to a stop in the muddy turf as Sheridan sweeps his hat, inspiring his fleeing soldiers to reverse course and follow him into immortality.

Perhaps after students have finished reading this "true tale" and have had the opportunity of visiting one or more of the locations associated with it, they can decide for themselves whether they agree with young Americans of an earlier era – who had no doubt that, once upon a time, an amazing animal indeed played a key role in saving our nation.

Prologue

The Blue Moon and the Hero

Do you believe in second chances?

Do you believe that animals can make a difference in our lives?

You probably answered "Yes" to both questions.

How about this: Do you believe also that, once in a *blue moon*, some special animal – such as a really amazing horse – could help change the course of history?

Well, whether or not you consider this a possibility, please read on. For what follows is –

A tale of a courageous four-legged fellow
Who truly became an American hero.

Chapter 1

Dark Horses

We all know that great countries like the United States need good, smart peacemakers in order to keep fights from breaking out. However, if peace fails and our country has to go to war, we need some good, smart military men and women, as well.

No doubt, General Philip H. Sheridan was one of the greatest military leaders that America has ever produced. He was a determined, energetic man with jet-black hair and dark piercing eyes – the kind that bore down on you like a shiny laser beam. Today, historians consider him to be one of America's most successful commanders in time of war.

However, he almost missed his chance.

You see, Phil Sheridan was pegged as *just* a good staff officer – one who performed important but oftentimes tedious and boring paperwork, such as filling out orders for provisions for the army and organizing the movement of troops and their supplies along rail lines and over muddy roads traveled by mule-driven carts.

During the first part of the American Civil War, the senior officers for whom Sheridan worked thought that he was much better suited to sitting in a chair behind a desk writing out requisition slips and getting tents and ammunition to the soldiers, rather than leading men into combat on the back of a horse. Phil tried and tried to convince his superiors that he was capable of doing much more; but he was turned down. He dreamed about being out in the field, at the front of battle, leading men. While many officers around him were given new opportunities and new promotions, Phil Sheridan just seemed to be stuck at the rank of Captain in the U.S. Army, doing important but behind-the-scenes paperwork.

Then, in May 1862, over a year into the American Civil War, Phil Sheridan's chance finally came, when the governor of Michigan needed a new reliable commander for one of his volunteer cavalry regiments. Finally, Phil's boss let him go from his headquarters job and take the position. Phil was clearly excited about being able to prove himself, and he was going to try as hard as he could to become a successful leader.

You see, no matter what he was doing, Phil Sheridan always gave his best; and he carried his long, full chest quite proudly to show everyone his confidence. Unfortunately, his legs were somewhat short. In fact, they were so short that, while his men always respected him, they affectionately called him "*Little* Phil." With his large head, long upper frame, and short legs, Little Phil at times seemed to look more like a Leprechaun than he did a great American warrior.

After meeting the rather bite-sized officer several years later, President Abraham Lincoln – who himself was often the recipient of hurtful remarks about his looks because of his tall, lanky limbs – even made a joke about Little Phil's seemingly mismatched frame. Lincoln described Sheridan as "a brown chunky little chap, with a long body, short legs. . . and such long arms that, if his ankles itch, he can scratch them without stooping."

Lincoln's point, of course, was that no one should be underestimated because of his physical appearance. Good advice.

Well, nothing was going to stop Little Phil from proving his worth! In a matter of weeks, after becoming the commander of his cavalry regiment, which was fighting in the northern part of Mississippi, he was given command over an entire brigade of 820 cavalry troopers. Shortly after this, Little Phil's outfit was attacked by an enemy force several times its size near the town of Booneville, Mississippi. However, Little Phil had done his homework. He had drawn detailed maps of the area, and he knew every inch of the geography around the town. He had thought out in advance how his troopers might defend their positions. So, to everyone's surprise, Little Phil's smaller force of cavalry achieved a decisive victory on that day, July 1, 1862.

Little Phil's success so impressed his superiors that they all called for his promotion once again. This time, he would receive general officer's "stars" to wear on his shoulders.

Absolutely amazing! Given this second chance, Little Phil Sheridan, in scarcely six weeks' time – having been presented with the right circumstances and having worked as hard as he could – moved all the way up from being a junior officer shuffling papers from behind a desk to commanding nearly a thousand men in battle. Moreover, he would soon become a brigadier general.

Little Phil's cavalry was then ordered to the nearby town of Rienzi (pronounced "Rye-EN-zee"), where they would provide defenses and conduct probing attacks in behalf of the large U.S. field army operating in northern Mississippi.

On August 26, 1862, just outside of Rienzi, Little Phil's forces beat back yet another attack.

Several days later, during a pause in the fighting, Captain Archibald P. Campbell, an officer serving under Sheridan in the 2nd Michigan Cavalry Regiment, presented Little Phil with the most amazing horse that the small commander had ever seen.

Captain Campbell had brought the horse with him from Michigan as a spare mount, but he had never ridden the animal in combat because he considered him too spirited – too unreliable.

Archibald Campbell adored the animal as a pet. However, since he couldn't control him when riding, he considered it to be no big loss if he were to give the horse away to someone else. He knew that Little Phil would probably take the horse off his hands and care for him quite well, because Little Phil seemed to really like the horse. Archibald had even let Little Phil take the colt out for a ride several times. For some reason, the horse always responded to Little Phil's commands.*

The three-year-old colt had been well cared for by Archibald. He had even tried training the horse as a cavalry mount – before finally giving up. Also, the

---

* In his *Personal Memoirs (p. 177)*, Sheridan said that Campbell probably had problems controlling the horse because "he had been unaccustomed to riding before the war." In other words, he had been a "city-dweller," and thus not a particularly accomplished rider. Sheridan noted as well that Campbell really seemed to love the horse. For about a year after Campbell gave Rienzi to Sheridan, he would still come over to Sheridan's headquarters in the evenings to visit the animal.

regimental farrier (a sort of a combination black smith and animal doctor) had been caring for the horse's feet and ankles, and had kept him well fed and groomed.*

The majestic animal stood over six feet tall from his front hoof all the way to the top of his large head. He measured "16 hands" (about five feet, four inches) from the ground to his shoulder.

Possessing "Morgan" blood lines, the dark, untested horse was related to the famed "Black Hawk," who had sired several racing champions. So he was very powerful and fast. At a normal walk, the colt could travel five miles-per-hour over long distances without tiring.

Some described the horse's coat as dark chestnut in color, and his head and neck as topped by a long, black mane.

However, years later, writing in his personal memoirs (or autobiography), Sheridan adamantly remembered his horse as being all jet-black in color – every inch of him – except for three of his feet around his ankles, which were white.†

Just like Little Phil, the horse possessed dark, perceptive eyes, which took in everything around him. Moreover, the horse appeared to show the same sense of determination displayed by Little Phil himself.

The horse always calmed down and responded obediently to Little Phil as the diminutive officer

---

* The farrier, a civilian named John Ashley, was so good at his job that Sheridan kept him on as his personal groom to care for Rienzi throughout the rest of the war.
† The reader is challenged to visit the horse's display at the Smithsonian's National Museum of American History in Washington, D.C., to see whose description is more accurate.

would approach him. The cavalry commander was an excellent, confident rider; and the horse probably sensed and respected those qualities.

Little Phil loved sitting on the tall, dark horse. The two were a great match! Mounted on the beautiful colt, with the rider's long, upper body enclosed in his bright blue officer's coat, Little Phil looked more like "Giant" Phil.

Just as Little Phil was given an opportunity to prove himself as a battlefield commander, the small but proud officer decided to give this unusual colt a second chance of becoming a reliable warhorse.

After riding the anxious and spirited horse on patrol for several more days, Little Phil had the feeling that this unique animal, if given the right opportunity, might become one of the finest cavalry mounts ever ridden. Boy, was he ever right!

Phil Sheridan would later describe his beloved horse as "an animal of great intelligence and immense strength and endurance. He always held his head high, and by the quickness of his movements gave many persons the idea that he was exceedingly impetuous. This was not so, for I could at any time control him by a firm hand and a few words, and he was as cool and quiet under fire as one of my soldiers."

Looking back, Little Phil thought that no one had ever ridden a more superior horse into battle.

Little Phil's friend Henry Greiner also noted the horse's fine qualities. He observed how majestically the animal would always carry Sheridan as he rode. He said that the dark mount, if urged by only a word from its rider or a slight tug on its reins, would effortlessly accelerate from a swinging gait to a fast canter, "with the ease of a cradle and the grace of an antelope."

Little Phil began calling his horse "Rienzi." The name was probably given to him in honor of the village in Mississippi where Captain Campbell had presented Little Phil with the horse, and where the new commander had achieved one of his first military victories.

Rienzi and Little Phil soon made a splendid team as they fought together in a number of battles. General Sheridan would always ride Rienzi while campaigning and leading his men into combat during the war. Little Phil admired Rienzi's intelligence, endurance, and energy. Most of all, he respected his mount as a valued American warrior.

True, Rienzi was just a horse. He might not have understood a number of complicated ideas, such as why violence was unfortunate for people, or how to plan military battles – things that human beings can often figure out. However, he clearly did possess the important qualities of obedience, discipline, courage, energy, loyalty, and reliability – characteristics which are essential for any job, whether one is trying to peacefully resolve an argument, fighting in a war, or just going to school. In a nutshell, Rienzi had good character. For all of these things, Little Phil loved his horse. He just knew that Rienzi was a winner!

Two years later, after Little Phil and Rienzi would win their greatest victory, Little Phil would rename his horse "Winchester" – but let's save that for later on in our story.

Chapter 2

The American Civil War

General Philip H. Sheridan and his horse Rienzi fought during the most horrific war in our nation's history. It was a huge conflict that broke out between our Northern and Southern states. It is known today as the American Civil War, and it occurred from 1861 to 1865.

The Civil War was fought for several unfortunate reasons. We'll go into more detail about these a little later. Let's just say for now that the fighting came about mainly because people living in different parts of the country lost their trust with one another. They were so firm in some of their beliefs that they became unwilling to resolve their differences by talking it over and trying to understand the other side's point of view. Instead, they just sort of let things get out of hand. Sadly, the two sides eventually resorted to violence.

In thinking about this terrible war, it's very important that we try to understand the perspectives of those people living in the United States over 150 years ago. Only then can we appreciate how this war came about, and why people were so determined to fight it to its bitter end.

Chapter 3

Differing Views of the War and Its Causes

The Southern Perspective

In 1861, one could sum up the "Southern" point-of-view by saying that most people living in the South thought that the Northerners – many of whom lived in cities and worked in factories – were getting too nosy in telling them how to run their lives and businesses. Unlike in the North, the economy in the South was based almost exclusively on growing crops, such as tobacco and cotton, on large farms called "plantations." The common folk lived on smaller farms. Most plantation owners and some farm owners used African Americans as slaves. Many leaders in the Southern states believed that the institution of slavery – which unfortunately had been in existence in the South for about 200 years – was essential to their way of life.

The Southern states in late 1860 and early 1861 believed that they needed to do something to protect the freedoms that their forefathers had gained by fighting the Revolutionary War, about 80 years before. This included what they believed to be an American's right to own slaves. Although many Americans thought that slavery was wrong (including many people living in the South), it was considered by the U.S. Supreme Court before the Civil War as a legal institution.

Desiring their independence from Northern interference – just as the American Colonists wanted independence from Great Britain – these Southern states decided that they had had enough of the North's meddling and asserted their sovereignty. After the election of Abraham Lincoln to the U.S. Presidency in November 1860, seven states in the "deep South" – South Carolina, Mississippi, Florida, Alabama, Georgia, Louisiana, and Texas – seceded from the United States in order to protect their way of life, including the institution of slavery. They formed their own country, "The Confederate States of America."

Several months later, Confederate forces seized and attacked U.S. installations in the South belonging to the Federal government (such as Fort Sumter in April 1861). As Southern patriotism rose due to these momentous events, and as President Lincoln called for Northern volunteers to form an army in order to invade the South and suppress the rebellion, four additional states – Virginia, North Carolina, Tennessee, and Arkansas – seceded from the United States and joined the other Confederate states in their "common cause."

The Northern View

Americans living in the Northern parts of the United States saw the problems quite differently. Just like Southerners, people living in the North were very proud of what our country's founders had accomplished in creating an independent United States of America. However, they believed that, if the Southern states were allowed to leave the United States, then many of the important rights that their grandfathers had fought so hard to establish would be lost.

Northerners considered Southerners as "Rebels," because they were thought to be in a state of rebellion against the U.S. Constitution by leaving the United States. Northerners feared that, if the Union were to split apart, this would foreshadow the end of the great American "experiment" in democracy.

In addition, there was growing sentiment in the North that slavery, although perhaps legal according to earlier Supreme Court decisions, was just wrong. Later on during the war, the idea of doing away with slavery throughout the United States became one of the main reasons for the North continuing with its fight against the South, along with preserving the Union. However, it was not the reason why Northerners went to war at the very beginning.

As the crisis over Fort Sumter came to a head in April 1861, many Americans in the North supported President Lincoln's call to form an army with which to invade the South. They fully agreed with the argument that, in order to preserve the American experiment in democracy, the Federal government in Washington, D.C., needed to force the Southern states back into the original country – that is, the United States of America.

To put the Union back together again, Northerners created armies and marched them south under the flag of the United States, called "Old Glory." This infuriated even more Southerners, who were creating their own armies about the same time. Southern soldiers, who were led into battle under their new Confederate flag, often called the "Stars and Bars," tried to fight the Northerners back for over four years. During the American Civil War, the two sides lost over

620,000 men who died, and many more who were wounded. Moreover, countless numbers of animals – including horses, mules, pigs, cows, sheep, and chickens – also lost their lives during the conflict.

Chapter 4

The Slavery Question

Northerners didn't like several practices that had been going on in the South for some time. In particular, an increasing number of people living in the North opposed the institution of slavery, which was still legal according to the Supreme Court's "Dread Scott Decision" several years before.*

Later, it would take a Constitutional Amendment – the 13th – to make it clear that slavery could no longer be practiced anywhere in the United States. Two more Amendments were required in order to recognize former slaves as full-fledged citizens.

Clearly, the strong disagreement over slavery became the chief *underlying* reason for the mistrust between the sides. This mistrust, in turn, led to the secession of a number of Southern states from the Union and the outbreak of the fighting in April 1861.

Unfortunately, the terrible practice of capturing and selling human beings for slave labor had been around throughout human history. In the centuries after Columbus "discovered" America in 1492, merchants began transporting captives by the boatload from Africa to the New World to work in the hot,

---

* The Dread Scott decision of 1857 also upset the various "compromises" that Congress had enacted in order limit the expansion of slavery into the territories. After the decision, some Americans even wondered whether the institution could legally expand as far north as the Canadian border.

miserable climates of what became the Spanish, Portuguese, and English colonies.

Regrettably, over the centuries, a number of European, Arab, and American merchants – and even several African kingdoms themselves – made fortunes capturing, transporting, and selling unfortunate human beings as slaves.

By the time that the American Civil War had begun, the trade in human cargo had been outlawed in many corners of the world – if not but for a relatively short span of time before the beginning of the conflict. It was illegal to import slaves into the United States. However, owning and selling human beings within and between Southern states was still permitted, and many people living in the South couldn't conceive of their way of life without the institution of slavery to support their economy.

Most of the Southerners who fought for their independence in the Civil War didn't own slaves. They were, by and large, good, honest, and hard-working people, just like most Northerners; and they were fighting to gain their independence from what they believed to be Northern interference in their local affairs. Unfortunately, many of them still held onto the notion that African-American slaves *could* be treated as property; and they were upset that many Northern states ignored the laws requiring them to return runaway slaves. Moreover, most Southerners thought that Northerners had no right to come down and tell them what to do with any of the property they owned, human or otherwise.

Initially, the North just wanted to put the nation back together again. However, as the war progressed, many people in the North, led by President Abraham Lincoln, thought more and more about the terrible practice of slavery in America. They decided that it was time to alter the purpose of the war against the South. With the Emancipation Proclamations (one signed by President Lincoln in September 1862, the other in January 1863), the North signaled that it would continue the war as before – to force the Southern states back into the Union – but that this objective would be broadened to eliminate the practice of slavery throughout the entire United States, as well.[*]

---

[*] While Lincoln's thinking about slavery evolved over the course of the war to the point of eliminating the practice throughout the United States, the Emancipation Proclamations (a preliminary and a final one) were executive actions that the President exercised on his own authority as Commander-in-Chief and not actual legislation passed by the U.S. Congress. The legal argument was that Lincoln was acting to deprive the South of its war-making capacity; therefore, the provision for freeing slaves applied only to areas of the South still in rebellion as of January 1, 1863. For example, the institution of slavery remained legal in Maryland – a slave-holding state – because it had remained in the Union. The passage of the 13th Amendment, the central theme of the Steven Spielberg film *Lincoln*, was necessitated because the Emancipation Proclamation was thought to be legally defensible only during the course of the war; and it was not applied everywhere.

Chapter 5

The South's Bold Plan for Victory

In the fall of 1864 – about two-and-a-half years into the war – Americans on both sides began to grow tired of all the fighting. The North's wartime goals of restoring the Union and doing away with slavery were still a long way off from being realized.

Hundreds of thousands of men on both sides had already died. A portion of the South had been devastated by Northern armies. In the North, fewer and fewer men volunteered to become soldiers. Men were being "called to duty" against their will, and riots broke out in places such as New York City in protest against drafting yet more men to fight in this terrible "meat-grinder" of a war.

While a good portion of the South was now controlled by the North, General Ulysses S. Grant, the commander of all Union armies, in the summer of 1864 found himself in a deadlock with Southern General Robert E. Lee, whose Army of Northern Virginia was valiantly defending the Confederate capital of Richmond, Virginia.

As the two armies faced each other in their newly dug trenches around Richmond and the neighboring city of Petersburg, General Lee decided upon a bold plan. He would pull a portion of his army out of the defenses around Richmond and Petersburg, and send them up through the Shenandoah Valley to threaten the Northern capital of Washington, D.C.

General Lee sent General Jubal Early and his forces to the north. However, having failed in his attempt to capture Washington, D.C., in July 1864, Early was forced to retreat with his army back southwest into the Shenandoah Valley. As the stand-off continued in the southern part of Virginia, Jubal Early managed to lead his men up and down the Shenandoah Valley in a seesaw of advances and retreats against Northern forces.

In October 1864, it was rumored that General Lee was about to reduce his defenses around Richmond once again, and send even more men to help Jubal Early.

You see, the Northern Presidential elections were scheduled to take place the following month of November. (Our Presidential elections today are still held every four years during November.) Lee figured that, if Jubal Early could win a great victory – or better yet, capture Washington, D.C. – then the Northerners might *not* re-elect Abraham Lincoln as their President. Without Lincoln leading the Union, the South believed that the North might quit fighting, and just let the South go its separate way.

A Northern army had captured the important Southern city of Atlanta, Georgia, on September 2, 1864. Many in the North thought that this important victory would ensure President Lincoln's re-election. However, popular opinion can change quickly – very much so during a national crisis, such as civil war. So nothing was for certain.

General Jubal Early knew that he had just one last chance to pull off a great Southern victory and upset the elections in the North. He planned to risk it all by making a sneak attack one fall morning against an army of Northern soldiers.

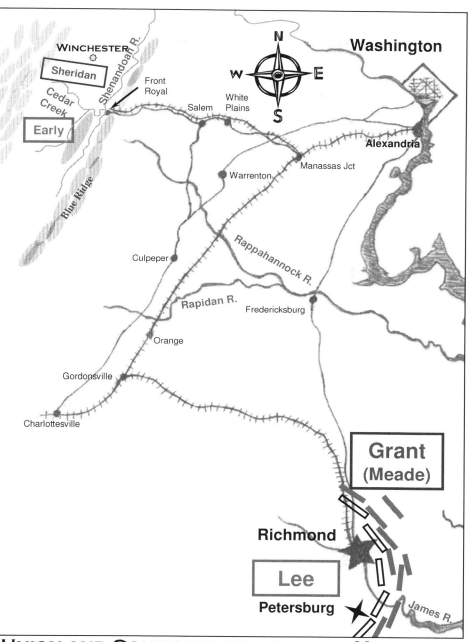

UNION AND CONFEDERATE ARMIES IN VIRGINIA
OCTOBER 1864
BY BRUCE D. SLAWTER

Most Northerners were sleeping in, because they thought that Early's soldiers had been beaten. These Northern soldiers were situated in their camps, which were located in the middle of the Shenandoah Valley on the north side of Cedar Creek, just a few miles to the west of its confluence with the North Fork of the Shenandoah River.

Early's intent was for his troops to quietly cross these rivers under cover of night. Some would travel by bridge, but many more would have to wade across low fords – and a few would even have to cross by walking right into the bone-chilling water, holding their rifles high over their heads. Once safely across, the Southern troops would attack the Northerners – just before the Northern soldiers would be waking up for breakfast at dawn.

The Northerners weren't expecting an attack. Several days before, they had routed General Early's cavalry at a place just south of Cedar Creek called Tom's Brook. Most Union soldiers reckoned that that the Southerners had scattered back up to the southern part of the Shenandoah Valley; and as such, they posed little threat. You see, solid information in any war about what the other side is thinking and doing isn't always available – more so, back then.

Around 8 P.M., on the night before the attack at dawn was to take place, General Early gave the order for the leading parts of his army – those soldiers on the right side, who had to travel the furthest – to move out. To avoid detection, these men would have to cross the North Fork of the Shenandoah River twice.

In between the two crossings, these brave but weary soldiers would traverse a narrow "pig's path" as they hugged around the north side of Massanutten Mountain. It was important that everyone keep out-of-sight, because there were still a few Northerners on the other side of Cedar Creek on lookout duty.

All of the requirements for a surprise attack were now in place for the Southern army.

Having launched events in motion, General Jubal Early, commander of the Confederate forces in the Shenandoah Valley, suddenly peered up, and with a look of worry on his face, noticed a dimly lit, nearly full *blue moon* rising through the mists.

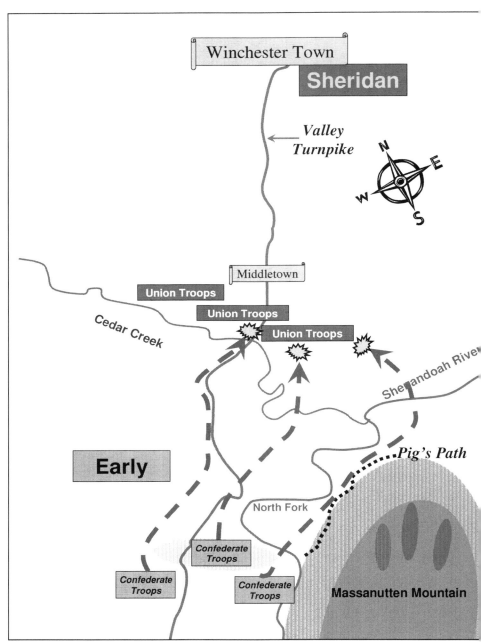

Winchester Town

Sheridan

Valley Turnpike

N
E
W
S

Middletown

Union Troops

Union Troops

Union Troops

Cedar Creek

Shenandoah River

Early

Pig's Path

North Fork

Confederate Troops

Confederate Troops

Confederate Troops

Massanutten Mountain

BATTLE OF CEDAR CREEK
7 A.M. – 19 OCTOBER 1864
BY BRUCE D. SLAWTER

Chapter 6

Waking Up to the Sound of Cannons

Several months after Little Phil and Rienzi had been sent to Virginia, Little Phil was made the commander of the Army facing General Jubal Early in the Shenandoah Valley. Little Phil's job was to protect the capital of Washington, D.C., destroy the provisions in the valley which kept the Southern armies fed, and eliminate Early's army altogether.

Little Phil was just returning to the town of Winchester from a conference in Washington, D.C., as the first group of Southern soldiers had crossed the first river and were winding along the pig's path, about 20 miles to the south.

Because of his long journey from Washington, D.C., a few hours by train, and a few more by horseback, Little Phil was particularly tired when he reached Winchester. He went straight to bed at the house of Mr. Lloyd Logan.

Little Phil intended to sleep in the next morning. However, shortly before 7 A.M., an officer standing on guard duty with other soldiers outside Mr. Logan's house suddenly woke up Little Phil. He excitedly told the general that he could hear the booming of artillery off in the distance down towards Cedar Creek. Dense fog along the rivers to the south hid the morning sunrise from view; so the officer couldn't see anything to explain all the noise.

Oddly, there were no messages from any of Sheridan's officers down near Cedar Creek. So no one in Winchester town realized at the time that the noise was the sound of the surprise attack being launched by Jubal Early – early that morning.

Little Phil tried to ignore all the commotion outside and go back to sleep; but he became restless. Fearing that something was wrong – and anxious to find out what was going on – he finally gave up. He ordered the cook to hurry up with breakfast.

Little Phil could now hear the booming of the artillery to the south, and the noise kept getting louder. He quickly dressed in his uniform, jumped into his boots, and went down to the dining room, where he gulped down his food much quicker than normal.

With a little sleep still in his eyes, but now fully worried, Little Phil ordered his staff officers (who often traveled with him) to mount up, and for a groom to saddle Rienzi. As he emerged from the Logan House, he quickly looked around for his warhorse. He would definitely need him in fine form today.

Little Phil, as usual, had nothing to fear – for Rienzi, always ready for duty, was standing outside the house, saddled and prepared to march out. As usual, the only thing to notice about the horse was that his tail was twitching nervously back and forth. That usually meant that he was on high alert. All Rienzi needed right now was Little Phil's command!

Little Phil still didn't know the exact meaning of the gunfire and the explosions. Oddly, there were still no dispatches telling him what was going on. He was going to have to find out for himself.

As Little Phil and his group of officers began their swift ride through the streets of Winchester and emerged into the open country, they could hear the church bells clanging nine times.

Chapter 7

Racing Up the Valley

On that day in October, as is often the case with fall days in Virginia, the air felt cold and clean, and the trees were wearing their autumn colors of reds, oranges, and yellows. On occasion, the General's riding party crossed stretches of slippery green grass, still wet with the morning dew. Little Phil could see the white vapor of Rienzi's breath steaming out of his nostrils.

Rienzi swiftly carried Little Phil along the brown, muddy turnpike, ahead of the rest of the riding party. As always, Rienzi was sure-footed and galloped in a smooth up-and-down motion.

Little Phil and his group quickly picked up their pace towards the sound of the fighting. As they raced up the valley, they could make out the sun rising over Massanutten Mountain, straight ahead of them. * The fog down by the rivers began to melt away, and they were treated to a spectacular scene of the beautiful Blue Ridge to their left and the Allegheny Mountains to their right. . . but they had no time to enjoy the view.

Barely a mile south of Winchester, the group reduced their speed to a canter, as they approached the crest of a hill on the other side of a stream called Mill Creek. Little Phil's face suddenly turned white; for he just about ran into a handful of soldiers fleeing

---

* The Shenandoah Valley rises gradually in altitude from north to south; so when Sheridan and Rienzi raced "up the valley," they were heading in a southerly direction.

29

back towards Winchester. They were retreating from the battle in disarray.

As he rode further south up the valley, Little Phil could see, to his surprise, that his army was rapidly falling apart. He watched thousands of little blue specks, his Northern soldiers, running back towards him in disorder. Little Phil could see way to the south that they were being chased by Southerners dressed in light gray and butternut yellow. Jubal Early's surprise attack was successful. Washington, D.C., and the Union were now at risk!

Expecting a second breakthrough attack by an even larger Southern force, Little Phil hesitated for a moment. He thought about turning around and heading back to Winchester, where he might rally his troops to make a last-ditch stand.

Alert to his master's reluctance to retreat, Rienzi stood firm as he faced the line of the enemy's advance. Perhaps – in just a blink of an eye – master and warhorse together sensed what had to be done. The Northern army *had* to make its stand on this battlefield, here and now, and not retreat one mile further back down the valley to the north!

Chapter 8

Turning Point Near Cedar Creek

Ordering several of his accompanying staff officers to dismount and form a line to keep stragglers from running off the battlefield, Little Phil and Rienzi, joined by several remaining riders, sprinted off toward the center of the running Northerners.

Little Phil and Rienzi suddenly came upon one Northern officer retreating with his defeated troops on foot. As he slowed down, Little Phil asked him what was happening. The officer replied, "General, the Army's whipped!"

Resuming his pace forward, Little Phil leaned over in his saddle and shouted in defiance as he rode past the officer, "You are, but the army *isn't!*"

Little Phil then spun around on Rienzi. As warrior and warhorse pranced around the field for all to see, the excited general shouted to the soldiers within earshot, "About face boys! We are going back. We are going to lick them out of their boots!"

Jerking his reigns slightly as he leaned back in the saddle, Little Phil was lifted by Rienzi straight into the bright blue sky. He then removed his cap in salute to the soldiers, as Rienzi held him in space for a brief second or two.

As horse and master came down with a thunderous clop, the men watching the amazing sight suddenly responded by waving their own hats in salute

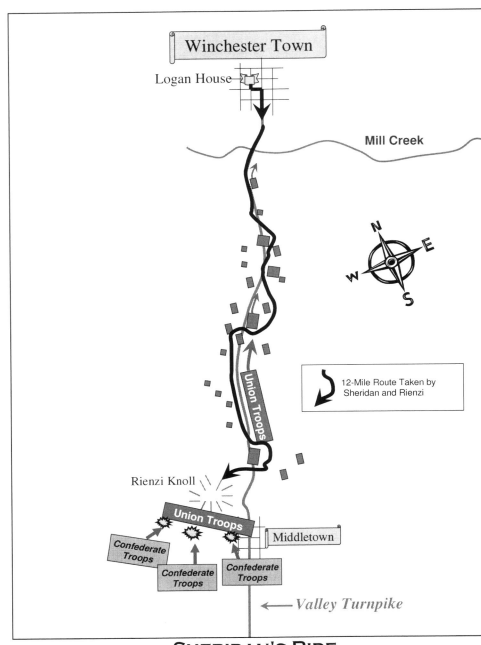

SHERIDAN'S RIDE
9 A.M. - 11 A.M. — 19 OCTOBER 1864
BY BRUCE D. SLAWTER

and by shouting "HURRAH! HURRAH!" – the favorite Union cheer back then.[*]

In response to these cheers, Rienzi began prancing back and forth like a beautiful circus horse. Never flinching from a difficult task, he then pivoted back around towards Massanutten Mountain and kicked up some clods of dirt as he started trotting back in the direction of the firing guns.

Anxious as ever to accelerate his journey to the front lines, Little Phil then tried putting his spurs ever so lightly to Rienzi's sides, behind the stirrups. But he noticed when he looked down at his boots that one spur had broken off. It had probably happened earlier back at the Logan House, when he was madly rushing to leave the town of Winchester.

Just to be sure that he could handle his powerful, spirited horse during this important phase of their race to the front, Little Phil asked one of the officers accompanying him to quickly break off a small branch from a nearby bush. Barely slowing the group's forward movement, the officer scooped down with one hand and tore off a small branch. He then quickly picked off the leaves and some of the little prickly barbs from it. Leaning almost out of his saddle with his outstretched arm, the officer then handed the switch to the General as they trotted along. Little

---

[*] There remains an honest disagreement between modern re-enactors as to whether the Union shout was "HURRAH!" or "HUZZAH." Many believe that a "huzzah" is just a term for a *cheer* and was not actually what the soldiers yelled. The author has chosen "hurrah" here because Thomas Buchanan Read used the term in his poem, "Sheridan's Ride," which he wrote several days after the battle.

Phil's idea was to use the switch as a riding crop during the rest of his mad dash across the countryside.

Little Phil had just barely brushed Rienzi's neck with the switch when the horse made a sudden lurch forward, almost throwing Little Phil backwards out of his saddle. The two then sped ahead of the rest of the group in a fast gallop; the others could barely keep up.

The switch really wasn't necessary. Rienzi, an experienced warhorse used to anticipating Little Phil's commands, didn't need much encouragement. He was always ready to do his best, and he had never failed his master before. One could imagine later on, as things calmed down after the battle, that Little Phil felt sort of guilty for having doubted Rienzi at all.

Inspired by the courage of the valiant general and his magnificent horse, Little Phil's fleeing men gradually regained their courage and followed him back toward the booming thuds of the Southerners' cannons. As they got closer to the battle lines, they could make out the distant rattling sound caused by soldiers firing their riffled muskets. Closer still, and the rattling turned into distinct pops – like a thousand fire-crackers all going off in a matter of seconds.

As the General's party pounded on, Little Phil glanced backwards over his shoulder. A half grin suddenly formed on his face, for he could see more and more stragglers turning around and following him back into the battle.

Little Phil and Rienzi rallied their troops in a similar fashion several times that day. Continuing at break-neck speed while racing towards the sound of gunfire, they jumped over obstacles and clamored around troops and broken-down wagons blocking their path. Finally, they reached an open field near the front lines of the fighting.

Throughout the ride, Rienzi could be seen skillfully skirting around trees and bushes and leaping over fences – just as if he were a modern football player, zigzagging his way past tacklers on his way to the end-zone.

Around 11 A.M., Little Phil and Rienzi finally reached the forward-most defensive line. It was held by a formation of Union soldiers who had not retreated in disarray.* They were crouching behind makeshift barriers, located just on the Winchester side of the small hamlet of Middletown. While most of the Northern Army had fled the field, these valiant men were courageously repelling the forward movement of Jubal Early's attacking soldiers. Little Phil decided that this would be the spot where his entire army would make its stand.†

When all was said and done, Rienzi, having demonstrated all morning long his awesome courage, agility, and endurance, had carried Little Phil across 12 miles of the war-torn terrain in just about two-hours' time.

Despite the choking smoke of battle, the bullets whizzing by, and the constant thud of cannon balls hitting the soft ground nearby, Rienzi stood bravely at his post while Little Phil re-organized his troops, bringing many who had fled the field that morning back into their necessary defensive positions.

---

* This formation was the Union's Sixth Corps, Sheridan's most seasoned veterans.
† Little Phil and Rienzi stood on a little rise on the battlefield known today as "Rienzi Knoll."

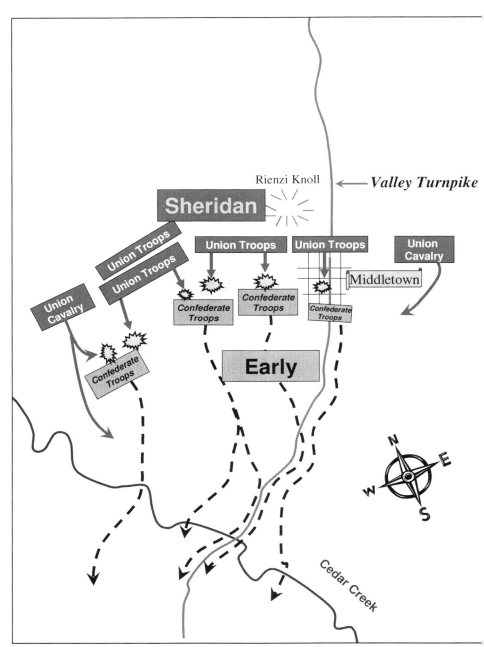

BATTLE OF CEDAR CREEK
4 P.M. – 19 OCTOBER 1864
BY BRUCE D. SLAWTER

Securing and extending his forces to his left and to his right, Little Phil and his men repulsed a probing attack by Jubal Early's army at about 1 P.M.

Then, after things quieted down a bit, Little Phil, sitting atop his proud mount, organized all of his returning units into attack formation. Sensing weakness in Early's line on the Southerners' left (the west side of the battlefield), Little Phil repositioned a large portion of his cavalry to his right. His thinking was to make a flanking advance in that direction.

As his men were getting into their assigned positions, Little Phil and Rienzi rode back and forth along the lines of Union soldiers, calling on his men to fight for their country and assuring them that they would be victorious that day. The "hurrahs" that they received from the Northern soldiers in return could be heard all across the valley.

Northerners and Southerners alike watched Rienzi and his master rallying the Union troops and getting them motivated for their counter-attack. Shots could be heard whizzing past their heads, but Little Phil and Rienzi never flinched. It was fortunate that neither the brave general nor his large warhorse were hit by Confederate sharpshooters that day.

Finally, with all his forces set to move forward, Little Phil ordered his decisive counter-attack at around 4 P.M. He had just a couple more hours of daylight to reverse the Union's fortunes. With a large portion of his cavalry on his right, Sheridan's army crashed into Early's men like a swinging door hitting a pile of eggs on the floor. Surprised by the bold move by the Northerners, the Southern troops were swept back across Cedar Creek and up the Shenandoah Valley to the south.

Jubal Early's bold plan, which seemed successful as the fog lifted earlier that morning, by evening had faded from view. . . just like the last red streaks of light retreating over the horizon with the sun.

Little Phil and Rienzi, both having displayed extraordinary valor and determination in the face of the enemy, had transformed the day! Together with the courage shown by many of their soldiers, their efforts ensured that the fight at Cedar Creek was one of the North's greatest triumphs, instead of one of its worst defeats.

Chapter 9

Battle Citations

Clearly, General Phil Sheridan's tremendous victory at the battle of Cedar Creek on October 19, 1864, sealed Abraham Lincoln's re-election to the Presidency during our nation's worst crisis ever. Lincoln's clear-cut electoral victory, coupled with the final attacks of Union forces the following spring, resulted in the defeat of the Confederacy and the preservation of the Union. It also ensured the final end of slavery in America.

Several days after the Battle of Cedar Creek, President Lincoln rewarded Little Phil Sheridan by making him a permanent Major General (two stars). Lincoln also heaped praise on Sheridan and his men by writing the following words: "I tender to you and your brave army the thanks of the nation and my own personal admiration and gratitude. . ."

Back in the Midwestern part of the United States, Shakespearian actor Thomas R. Murdoch, whose son had been killed fighting for the North with Little Phil's army one year before, asked his friend Thomas Buchanan Read to compose a poem about the momentous events that had just transpired at Cedar Creek. Read wrote the poem almost overnight, and he named it "Sheridan's Ride." The actor Murdoch then presented the poem during a dramatic reading at Cincinnati's Pike Opera House on November 1, 1864, less than two weeks after the battle.

Thomas Buchanan Read, *Philip H. Sheridan.* Smithsonian's National Portrait Gallery, Washington, D.C. Photo © 2014, Bruce D. Slawter.

Several newspapers covered Murdoch's presentation in Cincinnati, and the poem quickly "went viral" across America, along with further newspaper reports detailing all that transpired during the Battle of Cedar Creek. (One might say that the sending of newspaper stories over the telegraph back in 1864 was like the "internet" is for us today.)

By the time that Election Day came around a little over one week later, just about everyone in the North knew of General Sheridan and his black warhorse, and what they had both done to ensure a great Union victory.

Folks living throughout the country were looking for heroes during those gloomy days of the war – including Lincoln supporters working to re-elect the President – and both Little Phil and Rienzi just fit the bill.

Children across the North soon idolized the horse; and even the famed newspaperman Horace Greeley ran the poem on the front page of his paper, the *New York Tribune,* on the morning of Election Day, to help steer votes toward Lincoln. As a result of the Union victory at Cedar Creek and all the talk about these newfound heroes, Lincoln's election turned into a landslide.

Little Phil was surprised at his instant fame – and perhaps just a bit jealous at all the attention his horse was getting. However, he knew deep down that a large part of the praise did indeed belong to Rienzi. He understood that the North might have lost the battle had he not been aided by the strength, courage, endurance, and loyalty of his warhorse. Rienzi's performance that day was no short of outstanding! It was in many respects the key ingredient in Little Phil's efforts to rally his troops, put things back in order, and reverse the course of events.

Therefore, to honor his four-legged friend and to commemorate their heroic ride together all the way from the town of Winchester to the front lines near Cedar Creek, Little Phil changed Rienzi's name to "Winchester."

Little Phil and *Winchester* fought together in several more Civil War engagements, including the Battle of Five Forks, located near Petersburg, Virginia. During this battle, the horse once again contributed to a Union victory by displaying courage and strength while under fire.

Winchester also carried Little Phil to the final defeat of General Lee's army at Appomattox Court-house in April 1865. He was one of several horses to stand by in front of Wilbur McLean's famous house, while Generals Grant and Lee worked out the terms of surrender of the Southern armies in Virginia.

Epilogue

Remembrance

Winchester's High Honor

After the Civil War ended in 1865, Phil Sheridan stayed on in the United States Army. Based upon his proven track-record and outstanding service to the United States, this one-time desk-bound staff officer – who nobody thought was going anywhere – was eventually promoted to the position of Commanding General of the *entire* U.S. Army. However, Winchester, his famed warhorse, had seen enough of battle; and he was honorably retired from military service.

By order of General Philip H. Sheridan, United States Army, Winchester spent the rest of his life after the Civil War living in the most comfortable accommodations imaginable for a horse. The grooms and soldiers entrusted with taking care of this unique American hero always treated him as if he were a prince visiting the U.S. from some far-off kingdom.

Winchester eventually passed on in 1878. He was nearly 20 years old, which amounted to a very good life for a warhorse who had born the wounds and stress of numerous battles, like so many of America's wartime veterans.

Winchester was then given the high honor of having his body preserved and put on display in the Army Museum on Governor's Island in New York City. When the museum caught fire in 1922, workers managed to save the display, and Winchester was transported by ceremonial Army escorts to the

Smithsonian Museum in Washington, D.C. A band played old Civil War songs as Winchester left New York City.

Today, one can still view Winchester standing proudly in the National Museum of American History. Befitting a military hero of his fame, Winchester is located in the exhibit area called "The Price of Freedom: Americans at War." He is the only horse given such an honor in this important hall that chronicles our nation's wars.

The Costs of the American Civil War

Well over a million Americans lost their lives or were injured during the Civil War fighting for the principles in which they believed. Through their loss, we became one nation again – and we became a better nation. Slavery in America was abolished, and African Americans were recognized as U.S. citizens by several new amendments to the U.S. Constitution. Our nation began the long road toward mending fences between North and South. Racial healing – a much longer journey – began at the same time.

During the Civil War, Americans experienced the horrors of large-scale fighting for the first time; and we learned the importance of settling disputes between our fellow citizens peacefully.

Indeed, the price tag for the war, just in terms of the human beings who died, was extremely high – over 620,000 Americans. Many people, however, do not realize that over one-and-a-half million horses and mules also died or were injured during this terrible conflict.

Remembering Our Four-Legged Heroes

There are many memorials honoring the human beings who gave their lives during the conflict. This is quite proper; for we should never forget the sacrifices made by our service men and women during times of war.

However, there is one special statue which honors solely those animals who lost their lives in the service of our nation during the Civil War. It is a beautiful monument, located in the town of Middleburg, the center of Virginia's Thoroughbred country. The statue depicts a single horse with his weary head bent down peacefully – as if he were saying a silent prayer for his fallen comrades.

Tessa Pullan (British, born 1953)
Civil War Cavalry Horse, 1997, bronze

Base inscription: "In memory of the one and one-half million horses and mules of the Confederate and Union Armies who were killed, were wounded, or died from disease in the Civil War. Many perished within twenty miles of Middleburg in the battles of Aldie, Middleburg and Upperville in June of 1863." Permanent Collection of the National Sporting Library & Museum; bequest of Mr. Paul Mellon, 1999. The image, Copyright © 2014, Bruce D. Slawter, is reproduced with the permission of Tessa Pullan and the museum.

An equally fitting memorial to all of the "four-legged soldiers" who served in the Civil War is the poem written by Thomas Buchanan Read, *Sheridan's Ride*, which helped make Winchester known to the children of America. Here's a condensed version:

There is a road from Winchester town,
A good, broad highway leading down;
And there, through the flush of the morning light,
A steed as black as the steeds of night
Was seen to pass, as with eagle flight,
As if he knew the terrible need;
He stretched away with his utmost speed.

Still sprung from those swift hoofs, thundering South,
The dust, like smoke from the cannon's mouth;
Or the trail of a comet, sweeping faster and faster,
Foreboding to traitors the doom of disaster.
The heart of the steed, and the heart of the master
Were beating like prisoners assaulting their walls,
Impatient to be where the battlefield calls.

Hurrah! hurrah for Sheridan!
Hurrah! hurrah for horse and man!
And when their statues are placed on high,
Under the dome of the Union sky,
The American soldier's Temple of Fame;
There, with the glorious general's name,
Be it said, in letters both bold and bright,
"Here is the steed that saved the day,
By carrying Sheridan into the fight,
From Winchester, twenty miles away!"

As a veteran of 45 engagements, 19 pitched battles, and several bullet wounds, the horse called "Rienzi" or *Winchester* (his final name) is the most honored animal in American military history. For his distinguished service throughout the war, and particularly for the valor he demonstrated during the important Battle of Cedar Creek in October 1864, he clearly deserves the title of –

The Horse That Saved the Union.

*   *   *   *   *

Glossary of Terms

adamantly – in a manner that is absolutely certain

blue moon – "Once in a *blue moon*" is a very rare event indeed. A blue moon is an extra moon that occurs in a particular season. There was a blue moon or "harvest moon" at the time of the Battle of Cedar Creek.

brigade – a large military unit, consisting of two or more regiments

brigadier general – a senior officer who normally would command a brigade. During the Civil War, brigadier generals like Sheridan would often command a higher-level unit, such as a division. They wore one star on each shoulder.

called to duty – brought into military service, either because a person felt the need to join up, or he was required to do so by law

canter – a horse-riding term; faster than a trot, but slower than a gallop or run

cavalry – a unit of soldiers who would normally ride on horses. The cavalry often fought with swords, pistols, and rifles (some shortened, called "carbines"). Cavalry soldiers at times would ride to the battle area on their horses and then dismount in order to fire their weapons like regular infantry (ground) soldiers.

chronicles – records and explains

citations – pieces of paper celebrating the actions of people in the military; like a great report card

colt – a male horse that is less than four years-old

commemorate – honor, recognize, and remember as important

common cause – a term often used by Southern states leaving the Union in 1861 to explain that they were joining the other slave-holding states in order to fight back the Northern armies and maintain their way of life.

condensed – shortened, without changing the over-all meaning

corps – a large army unit consisting of two or more divisions (and many regiments)

decisive – clear cut; no doubt about what happened

devastated – destroyed; injured or killed

diminutive – small-like

dispatches – messages sent between military commanders

drafting – selecting men for military service who were not volunteers

electoral – affecting elections

engagements – military battles and skirmishes

exclusively – only; nothing else

foreshadow – seeming to make a prediction, some-
times in a negative light

fortunes – luck

flanking advance – attacking the exposed side of an
enemy formation because it was often its weakest
point

gait – a horse-riding term; the motion a horse makes
as he moves

gallop – a horse-riding term; a fast run in which the
rider and horse move up and down quite noticeably

hand – a horse-riding term; a measurement of the
height of a horse, based upon the distance between a
man's spread-out thumb and his little finger. Today, a
"hand" is about four inches in length.

impetuous – doing something without thinking
much about it in advance

initial – first; often the most important

landslide – clear-cut; no doubt about it

last-ditch stand – a final fight during a battle; the idea of military soldiers refusing to give up and willing to sacrifice their lives, rather than retreat. Soldiers often dug ditches for protection.

momentum – the movement of one's weight or mass

Morgan – a breed of horse used for coach-pulling and harness racing

obscured – unable to be seen

ominous – mysterious; bad

outlawed – considered to be against the law

pegged – pre-judged; placed (perhaps unfairly) in a limited category or group

perspectives – viewpoints; different opinions

probing attack – an attack made for the purpose of finding out about the enemy's strength and defenses. "Probing attacks" were not all-out attacks.

provisions – items an army needs to keep moving and fighting, such as bullets, food, wagons, and blankets

rallied – past tense of "rally," which is to encourage troops to forget their fears and get back into order; to inspire and re-organize

regiment – a military unit smaller than a brigade. During the Civil War, the "regiment" was the building block of the army. It was often formed from volunteers living in the same town or county. Ideally, when men would first sign up to become soldiers, a regiment would number about 1,000 men. However, as the war progressed, the numbers of soldiers in individual regiments became much smaller because of disease and battle losses.

repulsed – to have fought back the enemy so that he retreats

riding crop – a small whip used to control a horse

routed – defeated and scattered

secession (secede) – a state deciding officially that they were leaving the Union. The U.S. Constitution made no provision for secession. Southerners thought that it was legal, and Northerners thought that it was not.

Shakespearian actor – a performer specializing in the plays of William Shakespeare, the famous English writer from the early 17th Century

sired – having been the male parent of an animal

staff officer – a military officer working at head-quarters or in an office located behind front lines, who is doing necessary planning and organizing work

switch – a small branch or stick from a tree or bush

Thoroughbred – a majestic breed of horse developed for racing, jumping, polo, and fox hunting

troopers – soldiers who ride horses into battle and make up the cavalry

turnpike – a road usually built by businessmen or the government for which a fee or toll can be charged. Turnpikes were supposed to be built with solid materials and maintained in good condition; but more often than not, they were just muddy roads. Nevertheless, they tended to make for faster travel than local wagon roads or paths. The famed "Valley Turnpike" was better than most roads in 1864.

underlying – actual. A underlying reason is the real deep-down reason, not just what people said it was at the time or later on.

valiantly – with courage; bravely

volunteer cavalry – men who volunteered to become "horse soldiers"

Suggested Discussion Questions

1. What is the name of the Union victory that occurred on October 19, 1864, and why was the result so important for the North?

2. Where did the battle take place (for instance, what was the name of the region and nearby town)? Describe some of the area's features.

3. What unusual route did some of the Southern soldiers take to get into position before the battle, and why did they go that way?

4. What did "Little Phil" Sheridan and his horse "Rienzi" do in the battle that was so important?

5. What new name did Little Phil give to Rienzi after the battle and why?

6. Why did the horse become so famous?

7. At its most basic or simplest level, what caused the North and South to begin fighting each other in the first place?

8. What was the main underlying problem that caused Northerners and Southerners to become so suspicious of each other? (In other words, what was their greatest disagreement over?) Explain why there was a difference of opinion.

9. Was the institution of slavery considered *legal* or *illegal* before the Civil War? What's the basis for your answer?

10. What was President Lincoln's initial (or first) purpose for raising an army and invading the South in 1861?

11. What document signed by President Lincoln in January 1863 freed the slaves living in regions still in rebellion and also began expanding the North's purpose for fighting the war to doing away with slavery? (Hint: The President did this on his own.)

12. What legal document finally did away with slavery throughout the U.S., once and for all? (Hint: It has to do with the U.S. Constitution.)

13. What were horses and mules used for during the Civil War (you might have to use your imagination a little bit to answer this one)?

14. Why at first were Little Phil and Rienzi not considered the right individuals for fighting along side troops in battle?

15. How did Little Phil come to acquire his horse Rienzi in the first place?

16. Describe some of Rienzi's physical traits.

17.   What qualities did Rienzi possess that are important for anyone hoping to become successful, horse or human?

18.   Do you believe that Sheridan's horse really saved the Union?

Additional Resources

Primary Sources

Primary sources, such as documents, reports between commanders, and memoirs (autobiographies) written by the participants, provide exciting first-hand accounts and details of what the writers experienced. However, first-hand accounts in particular, which were often written right after the battles took place – or years later, after memories had faded (and perhaps to make some point) – need to be carefully compared with other information and sources that often become available many years later.

The following is a list of particularly good first-hand accounts related to the story of Sheridan and his horse Winchester:

Forsyth, George A., Gen, USA (Ret.), "Sheridan's Ride," *Harper's New Monthly Magazine*, July 1897.

Sheridan, Philip H., General, United States Army, *The Memoirs of P.H. Sheridan, Vol. 1.* New York: Charles L. Webster & Co., 1888.

U.S. War Department, *The War of the Rebellion: A Compilation of the Official Records of the Union and Confederate Armies, Series I, Vol. 17, Part 1: Reports, June 10, 1862 – January 20, 1863.* Washington: Government Printing Office, 1881-1901.

U.S. War Department, *The War of the Rebellion: A Compilation of the Official Records of the Union and Confederate Armies, Series I, Vol. 43, Part 1: Reports, Aug 4 – Dec 31, 1864.* Washington: Government Printing Office, 1881-1901.

One might also consult stand-alone documents, such as the various *Ordinances of Secession* written and approved by the respective Confederate states and Lincoln's January 1, 1863, *Emancipation Proclamation,* to understand a little more clearly the motives of the participants at the time that the documents were written.

Secondary Sources

Secondary sources, such as biographies of famous persons and histories of military campaigns, provide the reader with a larger context (or "big picture") of what happened, as opposed to reports and personal accounts, which tend to focus on specific events. These more extensive studies often take many years to research and write. Authors sift through a number of primary and secondary sources before they present their interpretation of what actually happened.

The following is a list of several good secondary sources related to our story:

Hayes, Rutherford B., President of the United States and Brevet Major General, U.S.V., "Grant and Sheridan in 1864: A Study in Contrasts," in *Battles and Leaders of the American Civil War, Vol. 5,* edited by Peter Cozzens. Urbana and Chicago: University of Illinois Press, 2002.

Morris, Roy, Jr., *Sheridan: The Life and Wars of General Phil Sheridan.* New York: Random House, Inc., 1993.

Stackpole, Edward J., *Sheridan in the Shenandoah*, 2nd ed., Harrisburg: Stackpole Books, 1992.

Wert, Jeffrey D., "Jubal A. Early and Confederate Leadership," in *Struggle for the Shenandoah: Essays of the 1864 Valley Campaign*, edited by Gary W. Gallagher. Kent: Kent State University Press, 1991.

Wheelen, Joseph, *Terrible Swift Sword: The Life of General Philip H. Sheridan.* Cambridge MA: Da Capo Press, 2012.

On-Line Resources

While they can change their content and location on the Internet, web sites covering the Civil War often provide new information or fresh perspectives. Some presentations on the Internet are also quite fun to browse through.

The Smithsonian's National Museum of American History has several interesting articles and presentations about Sheridan and Winchester on its web site, including a brief account of the horse's life in his own words. Go to http://americanhistory.si.edu, type "Winchester" in the search box, and then press on the "enter" key. You may even come across a picture of the display of Winchester in the museum, from which you can decide for yourself whether General Sheridan's description of his horse as being jet-black in color – except for three white feet – is accurate.

The web site for *The Civil War Trust* also contains a number of great articles about the Battle of Cedar Creek, including an entertaining rendition of Read's poem, "Sheridan's Ride," set to music. Go to www.civilwar.org, and click on "search" in the upper right-hand corner of the page. Type in "Sheridan's Ride from Winchester," then click on the search button, and you will be taken to a link to the music.

Answers to Suggested Discussion Questions

What follows are some ways that students, parents, and teachers might respond to the previous list of suggested discussion questions. Answers can be found in or inferred from the author's story. [Bracketed comments provide additional information not contained in the narrative.]

1. The Union victory that occurred on October 19, 1864, is known as "The Battle of Cedar Creek." By eliminating the Southern threat to the North (and to Washington, D.C., in particular), President Lincoln's re-election on November 8, 1864, was assured. Had George B. McClellan been elected President instead of Lincoln, he probably would have ended the war before the Confederate armies had surrendered; and we might be living in two separate countries today.

2. The Battle of Cedar Creek took place in the northwest part of the state of Virginia, in the Shenandoah Valley. The battlefield site is located just to the north of Cedar Creek, near the North Fork of the Shenandoah River. The Blue Ridge mountain chain is located to the east, the Allegheny Mountains to the west; and Massanutten Mountain can be seen to the south of the battlefield. Most of the fighting took place around the town of Middletown.

3. In between crossing two rivers, a portion of General Early's attacking army used a "pig's path" to get around the northern face of Massanutten Mountain. The route hid the movement of the Southern soldiers

from Union guards standing watch on the northern side of Cedar Creek.

4. Through their presence, inspiration, and forceful commands to retreating soldiers, "Little Phil Sheridan" and his horse "Rienzi" prevented the Union army from falling apart. Racing from Winchester, 12 miles away, they rallied their troops to return to the front lines of battle, organized a defense, and prepared for a counter-attack. Their personal efforts turned what appeared to be a Union defeat into one of its most significant victories.

5. Little Phil renamed his horse "Winchester" to honor him for his actions during the Battle of Cedar Creek and to commemorate their famous ride from Winchester to the front lines. Sheridan and much of the Northern public believed that the horse deserved part of the credit for the Union victory.

6. The war-weary people of the North were looking for heroes; and Sheridan and his horse fit the bill. Politicians also used their newfound fame in the campaign to help re-elect President Lincoln. Thomas Buchanan Read's poem, "Sheridan's Ride," written just days after the battle, was reprinted in many newspapers throughout the North; so everybody knew of their exploits. [Comment: After the war, the poem was posted in many American classrooms for students to recite. As with all sagas about heroes, some of the details of Sheridan's Ride have been slightly exaggerated. For instance, according to the poem, Sheridan and his "steed" rode 20 miles from

Winchester to the battle front, while the distance was really only 12 miles. However, historical documents reveal that most of the story is indeed true.]

7. At its most basic or simplest level, the North and South began fighting because the sides could no longer trust each other. They were so firm in some of their beliefs that they became unwilling to resolve their differences by talking it over and trying to understand the other side's point of view.

8. The main *underlying* reason for the suspicion between Northerners and Southerners had to do with their differences over the issue of slavery. [Comment: As students are often taught, there were other disagreements in the relationship, such as arguments between the states and the Federal government as to which should hold the most power (e.g., "state sovereignty"/"states' rights"), and differences over domestic expenditures and trade policy. However, most historians today believe that, had slavery not been in existence at the time, these other problems would have been resolved without resorting to war.]

9. Most people living in the North and South before the Civil War thought that the institution of slavery was *legal,* including the U.S. Supreme Count. [Comment: Although slavery was never specifically mentioned in the U.S. Constitution, its existence was inferred several times in that document, and Federal courts judged it to be legal in the states where it was practiced.] Nevertheless, increasingly large numbers of persons living in the North and some in the South

thought that slavery, although technically legal, was immoral; and they wanted the "highest law of the land" to reflect that thinking.

10.   President Lincoln's initial purpose for raising an army and invading the South in 1861 was to suppress the rebellion and force the seceding states back into the Union.   This remained his primary objective throughout the conflict.

11.   The Emancipation Proclamation issued by President Lincoln on January 1, 1863, freed slaves in regions still in rebellion on that date and began to expand the North's purpose for fighting the war to include the complete abolition of slavery. [Comment: Not all Americans living in the North agreed with Lincoln's proclamation when it was first issued. However, towards the end of the war, most Northerners had come around to the notion that the South had to be defeated not only to re-unite the country but also to end slavery altogether.]

12.   The 13th Amendment to the U.S. Constitution abolished slavery throughout the United States. [Comment: It was ratified in December 1865, about eight months after President Abraham Lincoln was assassinated.]

13.   Horses were quite important for cavalry units. [Comment: Many more horses and mules were used for transporting the tons of provisions required to support armies in the field. Horses were not only used by cavalry troopers while fighting, but they also

transported riders carrying messages and reports between commanders, scouting for enemy positions, and "foraging" (searching) for food and supplies.]

14. Little Phil's bosses initially thought that he belonged back at headquarters doing paper work, and that he wasn't particularly well suited to become a commander in the field. This was because of both his odd physical appearance and his reputation for attention to detail in his staff officer duties. Rienzi at first was considered by his owner, Captain Archibald Campbell, as too spirited to become a reliable cavalry horse; but Little Phil thought otherwise.

15. Little Phil received Rienzi as a gift from Captain Archibald Campbell while both were serving in the state of Mississippi. Although Archibald loved the horse as a pet, he was an inexperienced rider and believed that the animal was too difficult to be handled in combat. Little Phil, an accomplished rider with many years of experience dealing with horses, liked the black colt and believed that he would become a fine warhorse.

16. Rienzi was a tall, dark horse, and he stood about 16 hands (or five feet, four inches) from hoof to shoulder. He was very powerful and had great endurance. He could travel at five miles per hour over long periods of time without tiring. One observer remarked that Rienzi would speed up from a walk to a fast run "with the ease of a cradle and the grace of an antelope."

17. Rienzi displayed the qualities of obedience, discipline, courage, energy, loyalty, and reliability. In other words, Rienzi possessed good character.

18. Did a horse really save the Union? Well, you decide for yourself!

22053705R00054

Made in the USA
Middletown, DE
18 July 2015